Quiches are Supe

It's All The Ingredients You Need - It's All The Flavors
You Want

BY: Ivy Hope

Copyright © 2021 by Ivy Hope

Copyright/License Page

Table of Contents

Introduction

As promised, in this cookbook, we will give you an overview of the ingredients you should keep in the kitchen. You will be guided from my fridge to yours, also from my pantry to yours, or freezer to yours.

Overall, a quiche is made with pie crust and a yummy filling. In that filling, you will for sure find fresh eggs. Then usually some cream or perhaps sour cream, cheese and some veggies, meat or both. Some spices will be added and often some fresh or dried herbs as well.

Don't forget you can serve it warm or cold. To follow my theory of taking your time to eat and enjoy the quiche experience thoroughly, I think serving it warm is best, but I understand it can be a personal preference. Also, it can be served at any meal of the day, according to your schedule and lifestyle. Also, if you are going to reheat your quiche, please do not use a microwave! Use a toaster oven or a regular oven, and it will keep the crust crispy and avoid creating that extra humidity your quiche does not need.

Let's now come back to the list of ingredients you want to keep handy.

In your pantry: canned veggies. They are not as good as fresh or frozen ones, but they can be a last-minute ingredient, such as canned tomatoes, canned mushrooms, or perhaps even corn. Spices! You want to play with spices when it comes to quiches. Use some smoked paprika, cumin, Italian herbs, rosemary, oregano, basil, peppercorn, sea salt, garlic powder, onion powder, and more.

In the fridge, make sure you keep some garlic, onions. I often buy a bottle of minced garlic; it makes it easier. Keep the cheese you will be using, or perhaps always have handy at least Parmesan cheese, Mozzarella cheese, and Cheddar. If you have the chance to pick up some fresh herbs from your garden, make sure you keep them cool and ready to use. Of course, you will also stock up as season permits on fresh vegetables of your choice for the next quiche: leeks, broccoli, cauliflower, zucchinis, and more. Don't forget your eggs, the main ingredient of any quiche! Also, it is a good idea to have fresh cream and sour cream available.

Keep some staple veggies you can use to replace fresh ones in your freezers, such as broccoli or spinach. Also, you can certainly keep your deep pie crusts and get one out as you need it. I also find it helpful to store some fresh herbs you first seal if you had too many to keep fresh in your fridge.

It starts with a crust!

When you're thinking about making a quiche, you need to start with the fundamental ingredients. A crust is what I'm talking about. What is a better way to start with this basic recipe for deep piecrust? Of course, you can make more than one and freeze them as you wish. Try to follow the recipe exactly to get the best results.

Serving size: 2 pie crusts

Cooking Time: 20 minutes

Ingredients:

- 2 cups all-purpose flour
- ¾ cup unsalted butter, cold, shaved
- A pinch of salt
- 6 tbsp. ice water
- 1 tsp. cider vinegar

Instructions:

1. Use a food processor for this recipe. Add the flour, butter, and salt and activate. You should pulse into the mixture for about 15 seconds.

2. Stir in about 3 tbsp. of water and the cider vinegar. And pulse again for a few seconds more.

3. Add the remaining amount of water and pulse again together for another few seconds.

4. Remove the dough from the food processor and place it on a wooden cutting board.

5. Roll the dough into 2 large discs, and there you have it!

6. You can now use these 2 pie crusts to make 2 quiches. If you are not going to use them, cover them with plastic and refrigerate them right away.

Tomatoes and Finer Herbs Quiche

This quiche is so simple but so delicious it is pretty similar to a margarita pizza. It is essential to use fresh herbs for this quiche. It is also crucial to use fresh tomatoes. I often use grape tomatoes and cut them in half, so if that's easier for you. Finally, of course, you do need some Mozzarella cheese to make it as delicious as possible.

Serving size: 4-6

Cooking Time: 60 minutes

Ingredients:

- 1 deep pie crust
- 1 ½ cup mozzarella cheese, shredded
- 6 grape tomatoes cut in halves
- Salt, black pepper
- ½ tsp. onion powder
- 1 tbsp. fresh minced basil
- A little olive oil or butter
- 6 large eggs
- ½ tbsp. minced garlic

Instructions:

1. Preheat the oven (375°F). If you bought your pie crust from the store, it should already be ready in a pie pan. If you are making it from scratch, place it in a grease pie pan before using it.

2. Heat the butter or oil in a pan and sautéed the garlic with the basil for 5 minutes. Drain all the excess fat.

3. Place in a mixing bowl, add the eggs and all seasonings. Wish until the eggs are nice and smooth.

4. Add the mozzarella cheese and stir again.

5. Dump the egg's mixture into the pie crust and add face down all the tomatoes, apart from each other in the quiche.

6. Bake in the oven for 50 minutes and let it cool down before slicing away.

All Kinds of Veggies on a Quiche

If you like to collect the vegetables from your garden to create a very fresh and yummy recipe, this one will meet all the criteria you're hoping for. I love using zucchinis, red bell peppers, and certainly some onions and possibly some fresh herbs as you judge appropriate. The type of cheese used can differ according to your taste.

Serving size: 4-6

Cooking Time: 60 minutes

Ingredients:

- 1 deep pie crust
- 1/2 small, sliced zucchini
- 2 tbsp. diced sweet onion
- ¼ diced red bell pepper
- ½ tbsp. minced garlic
- 6 large eggs
- 1 cup cottage cheese
- ½ tsp. fresh minced oregano
- Salt, black pepper
- A pinch ground cumin
- 1 and 1/2 cup shredded cheddar cheese
- Some unsalted butter

Instructions:

1. Preheat the oven to 375°F. If you bought your pie crust from the store, it should already be ready in a pie pan. If you are making it from scratch, place it in a grease pie pan before using it.

2. In a medium pan on medium heat, melt a little butter.

3. Add the zucchini, red pepper, onions, and garlic to cook for five minutes. Set aside

4. In a large mixing bowl, combine the eggs, the cottage cheeses, and the spices and herbs.

5. Add the cooked veggies and stir well.

6. On the bottom of the pie, add the cheddar cheese evenly.

7. Dump the eggs mixture in the pie crust—Bake for 50 minutes.

8. Slice when it has cooled down enough.

Simple Smoked Ham Quiche

You can certainly, of course, use the type of ham you prefer for hi this recipe. I will choose black forest ham every time with no regrets. There will be a few onions, a lot of cheese, and eggs. This is our own edition of quiche Lorraine.

Serving size: 4-6

Cooking Time: 60 minutes

Ingredients:

- 1 deep pie crust
- 6 chopped Slices of Black Forest ham
- 6 eggs
- ½ cup heavy cream
- 1 cup shredded mozzarella cheese
- ¼ diced sweet onion
- Salt and pepper
- Some unsalted butter
- A pinch of ground nutmeg

Instructions:

1. Preheat the oven to 375°F. If you bought your pie crust from the store, it should already be ready in a pie pan. If you are making it from scratch, place it in a grease pie pan before using it.

2. In a small pan, heat some unsalted butter and cook the onion for three or four minutes.

3. In a large mixing bowl, combine the eggs, spices, and cream.

4. Add the chopped ham, Mozzarella cheese, and cooked onions. Stir again

5. Dump the filling into the by crust.

6. Bake the oven for 15 minutes.

7. Size in two small portions and serve while still warm.

A Flavorful Bread Like Quiche

This quiche is very different in shape and structure, but it will taste as delicious as usual. We will use the rectangle baking dish instead of a pie pan to extend the quiche to a much bigger surface. Also, this case will be crustless.

Serving size: 4-6

Cooking Time: 60 minutes

Ingredients:

- 12 eggs
- 1 cup of sour cream
- 1 cup of milk
- 1 cup of mozzarella cheese
- 1 cup of shredded parmesan cheese
- 2 minced green onions
- ½ tsp. garlic powder
- ¼ cup diced sweet onion
- A pinch of ground nutmeg
- ½ tbsp. dried rosemary
- Unsalted butter

Instructions:

1. Preheat the oven to 375°F. Grease a square or rectangle baking pan and set it at the side.

2. In a large mixing bowl, combine the eggs and the sour cream as well as the milk.

3. In a small pan, heat some butter and cook the onions for five minutes.

4. Add the onions to the mixture as well as the spices and the shredded cheeses.

5. Combine very well before dumping into the baking dish.

6. Cook in the oven for about 45 to 50 minutes.

7. Cut into squares and serve right away.

Cute and Tasty Egg's Muffins

If you are making egg muffins, you are making mini quiches without crusts. It is imperative to grease the muffin pan well. Now the content of the muffins will be simple. You don't want to overload them. The seasoning will be super important.

Serving size: 4-6

Cooking Time: 60 minutes

Ingredients:

- 8 large eggs
- 1 cup whole milk
- 1 cup of your favorite: cooked bacon crumbs, diced salami, ham or turkey, or a mix of all
- ½ tsp. chili powder
- Salt, black pepper
- 1 ½ cup Ricotta cheese

Instructions:

1. Preheat the oven to 375°F. Spray with oil a muffin pan (8 holes). Set aside.

2. In a large mixing bowl, combine with a fork the eggs, the milk, the cheese.

3. Add the meat you choose and the spices.

4. Combine again and dump equally into each muffin hole.

5. Bake in the oven for 35 to 40 minutes or until the eggs are solid and cooked all the way.

Chicken and Spinach Quiche

It is pretty unusual to use chicken in quiche, but this recipe will change your mind about the future use of chicken. I love using fresh baby spinach leaves in this recipe, and I also love using some cut-up dried tomatoes. Do not forget to use cheddar cheese in this quiche.

Serving size: 4-6

Cooking Time: 60 minutes

Ingredients:

- 1 deep pie crust
- 1 cup cooked shredded chicken or rotisserie chicken
- 2 cups fresh baby spinach leaves
- 5 eggs
- 1 cup of sour cream
- 1 cup sharp shredded cheddar cheese
- ½ tbsp. minced fresh garlic
- 1/2 tbsp. minced fresh oregano
- ½ tsp. onion powder
- Salt and pepper
- A little unsalted butter

Instructions:

1. Preheat the oven to 375°F. If you bought your pie crust from the store, it should already be ready in a pie pan. If you are making it from scratch, place it in a grease pie pan before using it.

2. In a small pan, heat some butter on medium heat, sauté the garlic, oregano, and spinach for a few minutes.

3. In a large mixing bowl, combine the eggs, sour cream, cheese, and all spices.

4. Add the cooked veggies, the cooked chicken and stir again.

5. Dump the mixture into the pie crust.

6. Bake in the oven for 50 minutes.

7. Let it cool down before slicing.

Blue Cheese and Mushrooms Quiche

I cannot think of a better match between cheese and mushroom than using blue cheese as an option. If you would like to add protein, beef would be a good one. I want to cut down the taste of blue cheese would another one that is not so strong, perhaps cottage cheese, or even add some heavy cream to your mixture.

Serving size: 4-6

Cooking Time: 60 minutes

Ingredients:

- 1 deep pie crust
- 2 cups fresh sliced button mushrooms
- 1 cup crumbled blue cheese
- ½ cup fresh heavy cream
- 6 eggs
- 1 tbsp. minced fresh rosemary
- 1 tbsp. minced fresh garlic
- Olive oil
- Salt, black pepper

Instructions:

1. Preheat the oven to 375°F. If you bought your pie crust from the store, it should already be ready in a pie pan. If you are making it from scratch, place it in a grease pie pan before using it.

2. In a small pan, heat the olive oil on medium heat and sauté the mushrooms with the garlic and the rosemary for five minutes.

3. In a large mixing bowl, combine the heavy cream, blue cheese, the eggs, and the spices.

4. Add the cooked veggies and even out the mixture after dumping it in the pie crust.

5. Bake for 45-50 minutes and slice away when it has cooled down.

Pesto and Mozzarella Cheese

We will use all the ingredients to make a fresh pesto sauce for this. This means that you need to buy or pick up from your garden some fresh herbs and mince some fresh garlic. You will add a little parmesan cheese to the pesto sauce, but you will use fresh soft mozzarella cheese for the rest of the quiche.

Serving size: 4-6

Cooking Time: 60 minutes

Ingredients:

- 1 deep pie crust
- ½ cup olive oil
- 1 cup fresh grated Parmesan
- 1 tbsp. garlic
- 1 tbsp. fresh parsley
- 1 tbsp. fresh oregano
- ½ tsp. ground cumin
- Salt, black pepper
- 6-8 slices of fresh mozzarella
- 6 large eggs

Instructions:

1. Preheat the oven to 375°F. If you bought your pie crust from the store, it should already be ready in a pie pan. If you are making it from scratch, place it in a grease pie pan before using it.

2. Add the oil, all fresh herbs, garlic, half of the Parmesan cheese, and spices in a blender.

3. Activate for a few minutes or until you are satisfied with the texture.

4. In a large mixing bowl, combine the eggs and pesto.

5. Add the rest of the Parmesan cheese to the bottom of the crust and dump the egg's mixture into the pie.

6. Bake for about 30 minutes.

7. Remove from the oven and add the mozzarella slices on top and bake again for another 20 minutes.

8. Serve and enjoy once it has cooled down a little.

Pepperoni Pizza on a Quiche

Is this a pizza, or is this a quiche? It is hard to tell because they are both delicious. They are both adding some of the most wanted ingredients in both, which is pepperoni slices. Let me see what else do you want on your pizza quiche. I love red onions.

Serving size: 4-6

Cooking Time: 60 minutes

Ingredients:

- 1 deep pie crust
- 6 eggs
- 1 cups shredded mozzarella cheese
- 2 tbsp. diced red onions
- 1 cup chopped pepperoni slices
- ½ cup pizza sauce
- 1 cup ricotta cheese
- 1 tbsp. dried Italian herbs

Instructions:

1. Preheat the oven to 375°F. If you bought your pie crust from the store, it should already be ready in a pie pan. If you are making it from scratch, then place it in a grease pie pan before using it.

2. In a large mixing bowl, whisk the eggs and the Ricotta cheese, along with pizza sauce.

3. Add the herbs, red onions, pepperoni, and cheese, and mix again.

4. Dump into the pie crust and bake for 50 minutes.

5. Serve with a side salad!

Onion's Quiche

I don't think there's anything wrong with making a quiche with the only one-star ingredient. In this case, onions are the star ingredients. However, because we want to keep it fun and interesting, we will use different types of onions: red, green, and white.

Serving size: 4-6

Cooking Time: 60 minutes

Ingredients:

- 1 deep pie crust
- 5 large egg
- ¾ cup whole milk
- 2 tbsp. diced red onion
- 2 tbsp. diced sweet onions
- 1 minced green onion
- 1 tsp. minced garlic
- Salt, black pepper
- A little unsalted butter

Instructions:

1. Preheat the oven to 375°F. If you bought your pie crust from the store, it should already be ready in a pie pan. If you are making it from scratch, place it in a grease pie pan before using it.

2. In a medium pan, heat little butter and sautéed the onions and garlic for 5 minutes.

3. In a large mixing bowl, combine all other ingredients.

4. Add the onions and mix again.

5. Dump the mixture into the pie crust and bake for 50 minutes. Make sure it's cooked before serving.

6. Put the hot sauce on the table for whoever wants to use it!

Mexican Quiche with a Lot of Jalapenos

This quiche is a spicy one. Typically, quiches are rather plain or perhaps more of a savory flavor. However, here all the spices and other ingredients will remind you of fajitas, tacos, or even nachos in a quiche. It is important to use some fresh sliced jalapenos to top it up. It will be beautiful and delicious.

Serving size: 4-6

Cooking Time: 60 minutes

Ingredients:

- 1 deep pie crust
- 6 large eggs
- ½ cup cooked ground beef
- ½ cup sour cream
- 1 cup shredded Monterey jack cheese
- 1 tbsp. chili powder
- ¼ tsp. onion powder
- Salt, black pepper
- 1 large sliced fresh jalapeno pepper

Instructions:

1. Preheat the oven to 375°F. If you bought your pie crust from the store, it should already be ready in a pie pan. If you are making it from scratch, place it in a grease pie pan before using it.

2. In a large mixing bowl, whisk the eggs and all spices.

3. Add the ground beef and cheese, sour cream mix again.

4. Dump into the pie crust and cook for 20 minutes.

5. Remove from the oven and add the pepper on top.

6. Place back in the oven and cook another 20-30 minutes.

7. Serve with salsa on the side.

Delicious Leek Quiche

Leek is a unique vegetable. Rosemary is going very well with eggs but also with herbs and cheese. So, they are the perfect ingredients to incorporate into a quiche. Here the leeks will be the star ingredients but don't forget to make the mixture for the quiche fluffy.

Serving size: 4-6

Cooking Time: 60 minutes

Ingredients:

- 1 deep pie crust
- 1 large, minced leek
- ½ tbsp. fresh minced rosemary
- 2 tbsp. diced sweet onion
- 1 tbsp. fresh minced garlic
- 6 large eggs
- 1 cup whole milk
- 1 cup shredded Parmesan cheese
- Some unsalted butter

Instructions:

1. Preheat the oven to 375°F. If you bought your pie crust from the store, it should already be ready in a pie pan. If you are making it from scratch, place it in a grease pie pan before using it.

2. In a medium pan, heat the butter and sautéed the leek, fresh rosemary, with garlic and onion. Set aside when done and drain any excess butter.

3. In a large mixing bowl, combine eggs, milk, and cheese.

4. Add the spices and cooked veggies next and combine again.

5. Dump into the pie crust and bake for 50 minutes.

6. Enjoy with a glass of wine, perhaps!

A Quiche Pie with Nuts and Feta Cheese

This will be a rectangle type of quiche. This pine nuts are what I prefer to use for this. And, you can cut the quiche into rectangles slices instead of triangles.

Serving size: 4-6

Cooking Time: 60 minutes

Ingredients:

- 2 cups crumbled Feta cheese
- 8 large eggs
- 2 cups heavy cream
- 1 cup chopped finely pine nuts
- 2 cups diced fresh tomatoes
- 1 tsp, ground cumin
- Salt, black pepper
- 1 tsp. red pepper flakes

Instructions:

1. Preheat the oven to 375°F. In this case, you will need to grease a rectangle medium-size baking dish and set it aside for now.

2. In a large mixing bowl, combine the eggs, cream, and spices.

3. Add the pine nuts, tomatoes, and cheese.

4. Stir carefully before dumping into the baking dish.

5. You should cook this egg pie for about 5 minutes.

6. Cut into squares and serve with a Greek salad, perhaps.

Beautiful and Flavorful Asparagus Quiche

If you lady asparagus just right on your keys, it will make a beautiful special quiche. It will almost look like a clock as the asparagus will tell time. I suggest you season them very well as asparagus can be pretty plain if not seasoned well.

Serving size: 4-6

Cooking Time: 60 minutes

Ingredients:

- 1 deep pie crust
- 6 large eggs
- 1 cup whole milk
- 10 fresh asparagus
- 2 cups shredded strong white American cheese
- ½ tbsp. smoked paprika
- ½ tsp. garlic powder
- 1/2tsp. onion powder
- Salt, black pepper

Instructions:

1. Preheat the oven to 375°F. If you bought your pie crust from the store, it should already be ready in a pie pan. If you are making it from scratch, place it in a grease pie pan before using it.

2. In a large mixing bowl, combine the eggs, milk, and all spices.

3. Cut the ends of the asparagus and make sure they are well washed.

4. Add half of the cheese to the bottom of the pie crust and the rest into the egg's mixture.

5. Dump the mixture into the pie crust—Cook for 20 minutes.

6. Remove from the oven and place the asparagus on top of the quiche as you put hands on a clock.

7. Place back in the oven for another 30 minutes.

8. Enjoy how beautiful it is before slicing and serving.

Bacon, Chives and Cheese in a Quiche

For this quiche, you should also use some fresh chives. As far as the type of cheese you need, I suggest using white American cheese. Because bacon is salty, you need to make sure you do balance it with some cracked pepper and a little bit of smoked paprika.

Serving size: 4-6

Cooking Time: 60 minutes

Ingredients:

- 1 deep pie crust
- 5 large eggs
- 1 ½ cups sour cream
- 2 tbsp. minced fresh chives
- 1 minced green onion
- 1 cup crumbled cooked bacon
- 1 ½ cups sharp shredded American cheese
- Salt, black pepper
- ½ tsp garlic powder
- ½ tsp. smoked paprika
- Some unsalted butter

Instructions:

1. Preheat the oven to 375°F. If you bought your pie crust from the store, it should already be ready in a pie pan. If you are making it from scratch, then place it in a grease pie pan before using it.

2. In a pan, heat the butter and cook for about 5 minutes the chives and the onion. Set aside.

3. In a large mixing bowl, combine the eggs and sour cream.

4. Add the cheese, spices, and bacon before also adding the cooked veggies.

5. Dump into the pie crust and cook for 50 minutes.

6. Serve with extra sour cream on the side.

Smoked Salmon and Capers as a Tasty Quiche

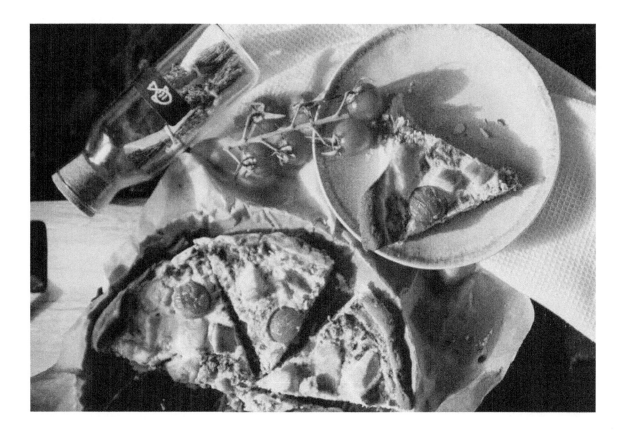

I do think that this quiche is fabulous. It should be eaten with a glass of Chardonnay or any other white wine you prefer. Or, if you insist, it can be eaten on Sunday as brunch food. You must use capers and some lemon zest to make this recipe just as fabulous as it can be.

Serving size: 4-6

Cooking Time: 60 minutes

Ingredients:

- 1 deep pie crust
- 1 ½ cup chopped smoked salmon
- 1 tbsp. Small capers
- 1 tbsp. Diced red onion
- 1 tsp. fresh lemon zest
- 6 large eggs
- 1 cup fresh grated Parmesan cheese
- 1 cup fresh cream
- Salt, black pepper

Instructions:

1. Preheat the oven to 375°F. If you bought your pie crust from the store, it should already be ready in a pie pan. If you are making it from scratch, place it in a grease pie pan before using it.

2. In a large mixing bowl, combine all the ingredients except the salmon and combine well.

3. Carefully add the salmon last before dumping the egg's mixture into the pie crust.

4. Bake in the oven for 50 minutes.

Breakfast Sausage in Quiche

I just think that pork sausages should remain a breakfast food. That is why using it in a quiche seems like the next best idea. My family loves this quiche. I will modify some ingredients depending on who's attending breakfast that day.

Serving size: 4-6

Cooking Time: 60 minutes

Ingredients:

- 1 deep pie crust
- 1 cup cooked breakfast sausage, crumbled
- 6 large eggs
- 1 cup shredded Cheddar cheese
- ½ sour cream
- ½ cup whole milk
- 1 tbsp. chili powder
- Salt, black pepper

Instructions:

1. Preheat the oven to 375°F. If you bought your pie crust from the store, it should already be ready in a pie pan. If you are making it from scratch, place it in a grease pie pan before using it.

2. In a large mixing bowl, combine all ingredients carefully.

3. Make sure you don't add too much salt as the sausage is already salty.

4. Dump the mixture into the pie crust and bake for 45 minutes.

5. Serve for breakfast, lunch, or even diner!

Artichoke and Just the Right Spices Quiche

I love artichokes. I love fresh artichokes, and I do like the ones you can buy in a bottle marinated. In this quiche, you will use both kinds. Make sure you use the right blend of spices and herbs to balance off the quiche flavors.

Serving size: 4-6

Cooking Time: 60 minutes

Ingredients:

- 1 deep pie crust
- 1 cooked artichoke (flesh from the buds)
- ½ cup marinated artichoke hearts
- 1 minced green onion
- 6 large eggs
- 1 cup cottage cheese
- ½ cup shredded Parmesan cheese
- ½ tsp. ground cumin
- Black pepper, salt
- Some unsalted butter

Instructions:

1. Preheat the oven to 375°F. If you bought your pie crust from the store, it should already be ready in a pie pan. If you are making it from scratch, place it in a grease pie pan before using it.

2. In a pan, heat the butter and sautéed the cooked artichokes and garlic for just a few minutes to make sure it takes on the flavor.

3. In a mixing bowl, combine all the ingredients together.

4. Next, dump the mixture into the crust and bake for 50 minutes.

5. Remove and let it cool down before slicing.

Fine Herbs and Sweet Potatoes Quiche

Is sweet potato pie usually served for dessert? In this case, the pie will transform into a quiche if you use the right savory ingredients. Fresh Rosemary will complement the sweet to me well, but I think adding a little nutmeg and cinnamon is essential.

Serving size: 4-6

Cooking Time: 60 minutes

Ingredients:

- 1 deep pie crust
- 2 cooked sweet potatoes or about 1 cup of sweet potatoes puree
- 1 tbsp. fresh minced rosemary
- 1 tbsp. fresh minced parsley
- A pinch of cinnamon
- A pinch of ground nutmeg
- A pinch of white pepper
- 6 large eggs
- 1 cup ricotta cheese
- Some unsalted butter

Instructions:

1. Preheat the oven to 375°F. If you bought your pie crust from the store, it should already be ready in a pie pan. If you are making it from scratch, place it in a grease pie pan before using it.

2. In a pan, heat the butter and sauté the herbs for a few minutes, set aside.

3. In a mixing bowl, combine the eggs, ricotta cheese, and herbs, spices.

4. Add the sweet potatoes puree and mix again.

5. Dump into the pie crust and bake for 50 minutes.

6. Serve as soon as it has cooled down.

Green Onions and Sour Cream Mini Quiches

These tiny quiches resonate simply. I just love the mixture of sour cream and green onions. When I pick some potato chips, I often choose those flavored with sour cream and onions or chives.

Serving size: 4-6

Cooking Time: 60 minutes

Ingredients:

- 2 tbsp. fresh minced chives
- 1 minced green onion
- Some unsalted butter
- 2 cups sour cream
- 6 large eggs
- Salt, black pepper
- A pinch ground cumin

Instructions:

1. Preheat your oven (375°F). Grease the muffin pan, 8 holes should be the right size.

2. In a pan, heat the butter and cook the onion and chives for 5-6 minutes. Drain all excess butter.

3. In a mixing bowl, mix the eggs, sour cream, cooked veggies, and spices.

4. Dump into the muffin holes and use a spatula to even out the small muffins.

5. Bake for 35 minutes and set aside to cool off before unmolding.

Broccoli and Sharp Cheddar Cheese Quiche

I do believe that quiche should reflect your tastes, whatever they are. I love broccoli and cheese casserole. I also love cream of broccoli and cheese. Now, I can say I love broccoli and cheese quiche. What makes it even better is if you use a little ground cumin in it.

Serving size: 4-6

Cooking Time: 60 minutes

Ingredients:

- 1 deep pie crust
- 5 large eggs
- ½ cup mild shredded cheddar cheese
- 1 ½ cup sharp shredded cheddar cheese
- 6 large eggs
- ½ cup whole milk
- Salt, black pepper
- 2 cups cooked broccoli florets
- ½ tsp. garlic powder

Instructions:

1. Preheat the oven to 375°F. If you bought your pie crust from the store, it should already be ready in a pie pan. If you are making it from scratch, place it in a grease pie pan before using it.

2. In a large mixing bowl, combine eggs, cheeses, and milk.

3. Add the spices and the well-drained broccoli.

4. Dump into the pie crust and bake for 40-50 minutes.

5. Serve with excitement to your family!

Zucchinis and Bacon Quiche

I love zucchinis in a quiche, but you should sauté them before incorporating them into the egg's mixture. Make sure you use garlic and possibly some onions. In this case, you will also use bacon then I decide on turkey bacon most of the time to keep the fat lower. Also, to balance all the ingredients, some cottage cheese is welcome.

Serving size: 4-6

Cooking Time: 60 minutes

Ingredients:

- 1 deep pie crust
- 1 medium diced fresh zucchini
- ½ tbsp. minced garlic
- 1 cup crumbled cooked bacon
- 6 large eggs
- 1 cup cottage cheese
- 1 cup shredded sharp Cheddar cheese
- ½ tsp. Italian dried herbs
- Salt, black pepper
- Little unsalted butter

Instructions:

1. Preheat the oven to 375°F. If you bought your pie crust from the store, it should already be ready in a pie pan. If you are making it from scratch, place it in a grease pie pan before using it.

2. Heat butter in a medium pan and sauté the garlic and zucchini for 5 minutes. Set aside.

3. In a large mixing bowl, combine the cheese, eggs, and spices.

4. Add the bacon and cooked veggies and mix again.

5. Dump the mixture into the pie crust and even it out before backing for 50 minutes.

6. Let it cooled down before serving.

Beautiful Shrimp Quiche

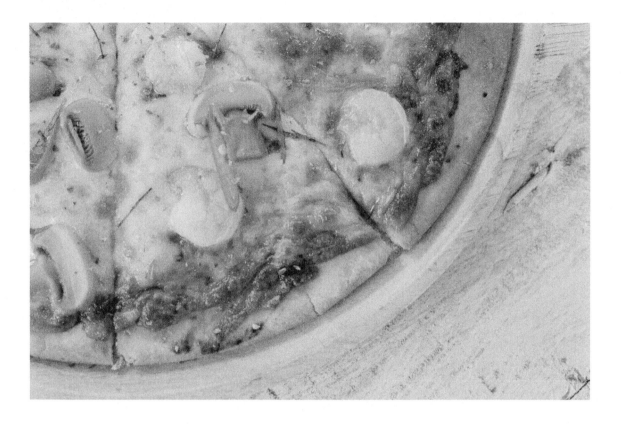

I am making a quiche with shrimp since I can ambitiously task. That is OK. I know you are up to it. You will need some medium-size shrimp in a lot of garlic. This case is also calling for promise and cheese, and you will not regret it.

Serving size: 4-6

Cooking Time: 60 minutes

Ingredients:

- 1 deep pie crust
- 1-2 cups of fresh medium-size shrimp
- 1 tbsp. minced fresh garlic
- 1 tbsp. minced parsley
- 1 minced green onion
- 1 cup freshly grated Parmesan cheese
- 6 large eggs
- Few drops of lemon juice
- Salt, black pepper
- Little unsalted butter

Instructions:

1. Preheat the oven to 375°F. If you bought your pie crust from the store, it should already be ready in a pie pan. If you are making it from scratch, place it in a grease pie pan before using it.

2. In a medium pan, heat the butter and sauté the onions, garlic, and parsley with little lemon juice. Add the shrimp and cook all together until the shrimps are all cooked or turn pink. Remove any excess butter.

3. Set aside.

4. In a large mixing bowl, combine the eggs, cheese, and seasonings.

5. Add the shrimp mixture and combine again.

6. Dump into the pie crust and even it out with a spatula.

7. Bake in the oven for 45-50 minutes.

8. Serve with cocktail sauce or perhaps even hot sauce.

Olives and Tomatoes Kind of Quiche

This quiche isn't Mediterranean-style quiche. The best type of olives to use in this case are calamata olives, but you can also substitute for black olives. Using tomatoes is a must. You can use fresh tomatoes, dried tomatoes, but just don't use canned tomatoes, please. You will find what type of cheese works best with these ingredients soon enough.

Serving size: 4-6

Cooking Time: 60 minutes

Ingredients:

- 1 deep pie crust
- 2 medium sliced thin fresh tomatoes
- 1-2 tablespoons of chopped dried tomatoes
- ½ cup sliced kalamata olives or black olives or any kind you prefer
- 6 large eggs
- 1 cup crumbled Feta cheese
- ½ tbsp. shredded Mozzarella cheese
- 2 tbsp. diced red onions
- ½ cup whole milk
- ½ tsp. ground cumin
- ¼ tsp. garlic powder
- Salt, black pepper
- Little olive oil

Instructions:

1. Preheat the oven to 375°F. If you bought your pie crust from the store, it should already be ready in a pie pan. If you are making it from scratch, place it in a grease pie pan before using it.

2. In a small pan, heat the oil and sauté the onions for a few minutes, set aside.

3. In a large mixing bowl, combine the eggs, milk, and all spices.

4. Add the dried tomatoes and olives.

5. Add the onions next and cheeses. Dump the mixtures into the pie crust.

6. Bake for 30 minutes and remove from the oven.

7. Add the fresh tomatoes and season with salt and pepper on top and bake again for another 15 minutes.

8. Serve with a side salad.

Conclusion

This conclusion will be a mix-match of information. Some fun, some useful, some crucial to the success of your next culinary experience in the kitchen, especially when it comes to quiche!

You may wonder if eating quiche is a healthy choice? It all depends on what you put in it, I would say! But in general, the eggs will provide you B12 and good cholesterol, iron, calcium, and zinc.

Also, your quiche will, of course, include some cheese of some sort. If you choose low-fat cheese, you will avoid high-fat content but keep the nutritional value of cheeses. This means you can stock up on calcium and many vitamins such as Vitamin A, D, Vitamin E, Vitamin K, Vitamin B12, B6, and C. Among minerals, you will also be happy to get thiamin, riboflavin, niacin in some exciting qualities.

Try to use some dark leafy vegetables as opposed to scratchy ones. They are rich in vitamins, minerals and they provide an excellent number of antioxidants., This way, you will protect your heart's health and lower your cholesterol.

Now, let's see how you are doing making your quiche?

Does your quiche seem to be runny at times? This means it may not be cooked enough. Keep it a little longer in the oven and reduce the overall temperature next time so it can cook slower.

What is a nice side dish to serve with a quiche?

It depends on your tastes, but here are some ideas: a salad, a potato salad, a macaroni salad, some sliced tomatoes with balsamic vinegar, a soup. If you prepared a vegetarian quiche, add a few slices of salami on the side, olives, or even sliced avocados.

Finally, what is my secret to a perfect quiche?

- Make sure you cook it for a long time and at even medium temperature. Plan a good hour to make and bake a quiche, as a minimum.

- Sauté the garlic and onions before adding them to the mixture.

- Do not skip the spices and herbs. You need a little punch!

- Carefully pick your pie crust.

Enjoy making your next quiche, and especially sharing it with friends and family!

About the Author

Ivy's mission is to share her recipes with the world. Even though she is not a professional cook she has always had that flair toward cooking. Her hands create magic. She can make even the simplest recipe tastes superb. Everyone who has tried her food has astounding their compliments was what made her think about writing recipes.

She wanted everyone to have a taste of her creations aside from close family and friends. So, deciding to write recipes was her winning decision. She isn't interested in popularity, but how many people have her recipes reached and touched people. Each recipe in her cookbooks is special and has a special meaning in her life. This means that each recipe is created with attention and love. Every ingredient carefully picked, every combination tried and tested.

Her mission started on her birthday about 9 years ago, when her guests couldn't stop prizing the food on the table. The next thing she did was organizing an event where chefs from restaurants were tasting her recipes. This event gave her the courage to start spreading her recipes.

She has written many cookbooks and she is still working on more. There is no end in the art of cooking; all you need is inspiration, love, and dedication.

Author's Afterthoughts

I am thankful for downloading this book and taking the time to read it. I know that you have learned a lot and you had a great time reading it. Writing books is the best way to share the skills I have with your and the best tips too.

I know that there are many books and choosing my book is amazing. I am thankful that you stopped and took time to decide. You made a great decision and I am sure that you enjoyed it.

I will be even happier if you provide honest feedback about my book. Feedbacks helped by growing and they still do. They help me to choose better content and new ideas. So, maybe your feedback can trigger an idea for my next book.

Thank you again

Sincerely

Ivy Hope

Printed in Great Britain
by Amazon